# My Little Gold

# PRIDE

MW01256355

By Kyle Lukoff
Illustrated by Michelle Jing Chan

A GOLDEN BOOK • NEW YORK

Educators and librarians, for a variety of teaching tools, visit us at RHTeachersLibrarians.com
Library of Congress Control Number: 2024940873
ISBN 978-0-593-80785-9 (trade) — ISBN 978-0-593-80786-6 (ebook)
Printed in the United States of America
10 9 8 7 6 5 4 3 2 1

**Rainbows** are everywhere!

You've probably seen big rainbows in the sky. Maybe you've noticed tiny rainbows shimmering in soap bubbles or shining in dewdrops.

But have you ever seen rainbows marching down the street?

When rainbow flags wave everywhere in a city or a town, it's probably time for Pride!

Pride parades celebrate the LGBTQIA+ community.

Pride celebrations are a reminder for everyone to be proud of who they are.

For a long time, LGBTQ people were made to feel
ashamed or embarrassed about being gay. There were even
laws that made it illegal to be gay.

In the sixties, in New York City's Greenwich Village,
police would arrest men for dancing with other men, women
for dancing with other women, and transgender people for
wearing clothes that made them feel good. But one night
in 1969, at a place called the Stonewall Inn, everyone
decided to fight back. Friends and strangers came to help.
They protested for many nights, telling the world that they
deserved to be treated better. The first Pride parades were
held on the anniversary of the Stonewall rebellion.

Almost ten years later, queer activists in San Francisco wanted to create a symbol for the gay rights movement. Designer Gilbert Baker talked to his friends about what it should be. One night at a dance, he noticed that his community was made up of all different ages and sizes and colors and genders. While spinning on the dance floor, the colors in the room looked like a rainbow. Gilbert decided that a rainbow flag would be the perfect symbol of hope for LGBTQIA+ people.

The first rainbow flags had eight stripes. Today, you might see many different flags waved at a Pride parade. The most common rainbow flag has six stripes, and each color tells a story.

**Red** is for *life.*

It's important to know who you are. Sometimes young people understand that they are queer or transgender or intersex. Some people take many, many years to figure out where they fit in. But all LGBTQIA people deserve to have full, happy lives with friendships and families and love.

**Orange** is for *healing*.

It's not always easy to be in the LGBTQIA community. Sometimes people are hurt or left out because of their identities. Finding support from people who share your experience can make you feel better. Helping each other heal is an important part of pride.

**Yellow** is for *sunlight*.

When someone keeps their LGBTQ identity a secret, that's called being "in the closet." Closets are small, dark places. There isn't a lot of room to move around. "Coming out of the closet" means being out in the light. Under the sun, sky, and clouds, people can grow with pride.

NOT GONNA HIDE MY PRIDE!

PROTECT TRANS ♡ KIDS ♡

SHOW UP FOR TRANS KIDS

TRANS ⚧ FUTURES

SA GAY

**Green** is for *nature.*

Queer people are everywhere. They live in every town
and every country. They can be farmers and swimmers
and scientists. They have pets, babies,
partners, parents, and siblings.
This earth has enough
room for everyone.

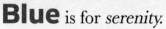

**Blue** is for *serenity.*

The world is a big, noisy place. It can feel extra noisy and extra scary for people who are gay or transgender or intersex. Serenity means being at peace by listening, breathing, and finding harmony with many different people.

## **Purple** is for *spirit*.

Pride parades are full of energy and joy. There's music and art and laughter and parties. There's fashion, food, and fun! Spirit means expressing yourself and being part of something big and magical.

Pride is celebrated all over the world. National LGBTQIA+ Pride Month is June, but there are Pride events held throughout the year. You can go to a Pride parade where you live. Or you can work with other people to start one in your neighborhood!

There will always be rainbows.
And there will always be **Pride!**

## A Note for Parents

Below are some age-appropriate suggestions for how to define each letter in the **LGBTQIA** initialism, but feel free to explain it however you feel is best.

**Lesbian:** Women who love other women.

**Gay:** People who are attracted to others of the same gender. Also used to describe men who love other men.

**Bisexual:** People who can love more than one gender.

**Transgender:** Someone whose gender is different than the one people thought they were when they were born.

**Queer:** A word that can refer to the many ways someone can be and love.

**Intersex:** Different ways a body can be, beyond just male or female.

**Asexual:** Someone who might not feel attracted to anyone in a physical way.